YORKSHIRE

CONTENTS

MYRIAD
LONDON

Wensleydale

The largest of the Dales, this broad sweeping northern valley boasts some of the region's finest scenery.

The Yorkshire Dales National Park, which straddles the Pennines, is an area of outstanding natural beauty where pretty villages nestle amidst the typical Dales scenery of drystone walls, barns and stark limestone escarpments. The grandeur of the Three Peaks, the scenic Settle to Carlisle railway line and the outstanding limestone scenery of Malhamdale are all to be found in this region.

HAWES The busy market town of Hawes sits between high fells at the head of Wensleydale, on the trans-Pennine A684 that links Northallerton in North Yorkshire to Kendal in Cumbria. Known as the "little capital" of Upper Wensleydale it is Yorkshire's highest market town. Local industries include the unusual Hawes Ropeworks and the Wensleydale Creamery where the famous Wensleydale cheese is produced. The

HARDRAW The village of Hardraw lies among spectacular scenery (below) almost at the foot of Buttertubs Pass – a link road over the fells from Wensleydale to Thwaite in Swaledale. The village is a stopping off point for walkers on the Pennine Way or those embarking on the ascent of nearby Great Shunner Fell, a bleak and remote summit which, at 2,349ft (716m) offers (in good weather!) spectacular views of the Three Peaks, Wensleydale and Swaledale. The jewel in the crown at Hardraw is the 96ft (29m) waterfall, Hardraw Force (above left) said to be the highest in England. Hardraw Force can only be reached by paying a small access fee and going through the Green Dragon Inn in the centre of the village, then walking a short distance along the banks of Fossdale Gill. It is possible to walk behind the shimmering cascade but only the most intrepid of visitors will attempt this feat.

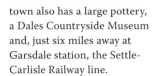

town also has a large pottery, a Dales Countryside Museum and, just six miles away at Garsdale station, the Settle-Carlisle Railway line.

BAINBRIDGE Set in the heart of Wensleydale, Bainbridge (above) has a wide village green with ancient stocks. The village is overlooked from the east by the remains of a Roman settlement. The horn hanging in the Rose and Crown Inn on the village green is a reminder of the time when the great forest of Wensleydale dominated the area. Each evening the Bainbridge hornblower would sound his horn to guide forest workers and travellers back to the village. The custom continues to this day – every year the horn is sounded at 10pm from September 27 (the Feast of the Holy Rood), until Shrove Tuesday. You can walk along the river Bain (the shortest river in England) which drains in nearby Semerwater. The surrounding area is well known for its hay meadows, pastures and stone buildings (left and above left).

GAYLE Just south of Hawes, Gayle (below) is sited at the foot of Sleddale. Duerley Beck cascades over a series of limestone steps in the centre of the village before rushing below a packhorse bridge. Early spring showers often swell the beck causing a torrent of foaming water to race past the rows of terraced cottages sited on the bank (left). A stone-flagged causeway leads gently down across meadows to Hawes church. Gayle Mill, situated just downstream from the main bridge dates from 1776 and has almost all of its working machinery in place. The building houses the world's oldest operating water turbine. The building operated first as a cotton mill and then, for the last 100 years of its life, as a sawmill.

ASKRIGG Just one mile north-east of Bainbridge on the northern side of Wensleydale, Askrigg (above) is a tiny settlement best known as the setting for the highly popular television series *All Creatures Great and Small*. Above the village sits Askrigg Common and beyond it the unmistakable form of Addlebrough. Askrigg was a former medieval market town and is now a haven for walkers and daytrippers.

WEST BURTON One mile south of Aysgarth at the northern end of Bishopsdale, the pretty, unspoiled village of West Burton has a large village green surrounded by traditional Dales' stone cottages, originally constructed to house workers in local leadmines. The village stands at the confluence of three valleys – Wensleydale, Bishopdale and Walden Dale. High fells rise sharply to give the village a spectacular setting. The annual May Fair, held on the green (left) draws large crowds. To the east of the village, the glorious West Burton Falls (below left) known locally as Cauldron Falls, are best seen from the footbridge at the north end of the village. After heavy rainfall, the falls quickly change from a quiet and picturesque waterfall to a raging and forceful torrent as Walden Beck fills with rainwater. The waterfall is one of the sights drawn by the famous artist JMW Turner during his tour of the north of England in the 1790s.

AYSGARTH FALLS Situated seven miles west of Leyburn, Aysgarth is best known for the spectacular waterfalls (right) on the river Ure that cascade down a series of large limestone steps. Riverside walks link the Upper, Middle and Lower Falls which are all within a mile of each other. The best view of the Upper Force is from the 16th century bridge in the centre of the village. St Andrew's church, just a short stroll from the falls, has a four-acre churchyard – reputedly the largest in Britain. The rood screen (left), carved by the Ripon School of Carvers in 1506, is said to have been taken from Jervaulx Abbey after its dissolution.

CASTLE BOLTON The small village of Castle Bolton, five miles west of Leyburn, is dominated by Bolton Castle (right). This massive fortress has loomed over Wensleydale since 1379 and is one of the country's best preserved castles; Mary Queen of Scots was imprisoned here in 1568 and 1569. In the middle of the village is a wide green and St Oswald's, the attractive 14th century church, which nestles in the shadow of the castle. The unusual wrought-iron gate (below) stands close to the church. Two of the castle gardens, the Herb Garden and the walled garden, have been restored along medieval lines.

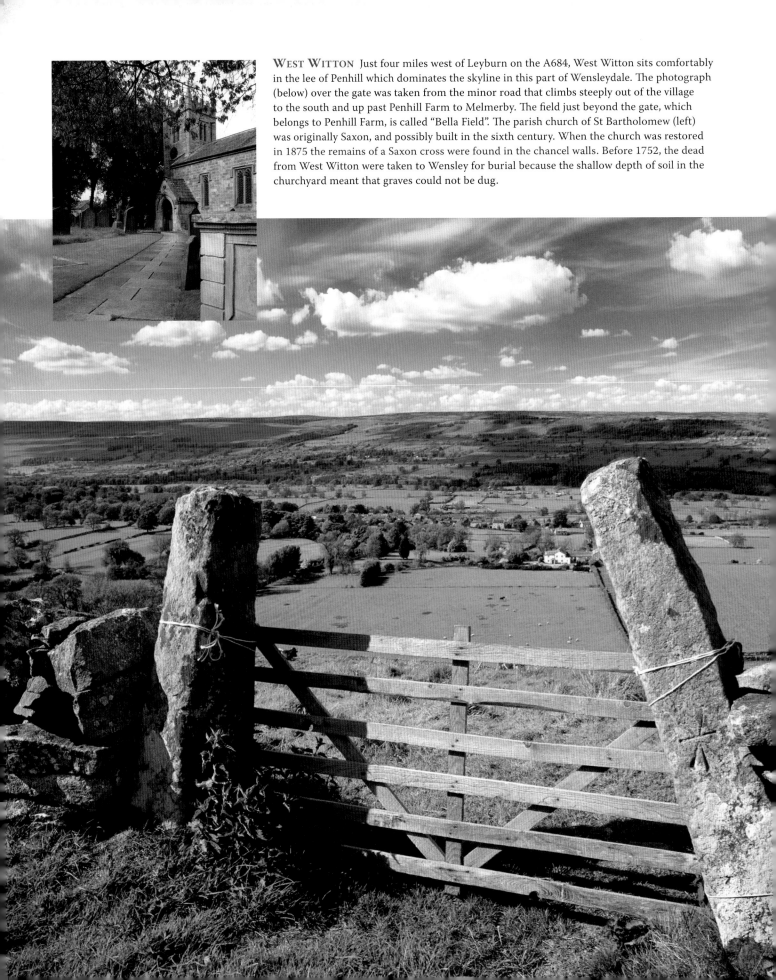

WEST WITTON Just four miles west of Leyburn on the A684, West Witton sits comfortably in the lee of Penhill which dominates the skyline in this part of Wensleydale. The photograph (below) over the gate was taken from the minor road that climbs steeply out of the village to the south and up past Penhill Farm to Melmerby. The field just beyond the gate, which belongs to Penhill Farm, is called "Bella Field". The parish church of St Bartholomew (left) was originally Saxon, and possibly built in the sixth century. When the church was restored in 1875 the remains of a Saxon cross were found in the chancel walls. Before 1752, the dead from West Witton were taken to Wensley for burial because the shallow depth of soil in the churchyard meant that graves could not be dug.

MIDDLEHAM Another local village dominated by its castle is Middleham (left and below), situated just two miles from Leyburn between Coverdale and Wensleydale. This impressive defensive structure is now largely roofless but almost all of the walls remain. The castle was built around 1170 by Robert Fitz Randolph during the reign of Henry II and was a fortress of the powerful Neville family, Earls of Westmorland and Warwick. The castle was the childhood home of Richard III. The massive central keep has 12ft (3.5m) thick walls and is one of the largest in England. The town has two cobbled squares and boasts a number of elegant Georgian buildings. The countryside around Middleham has been a centre for the training of racehorses for over 200 years and the surrounding moorland has many gallops.

Dentdale & Ribblesdale

These two western Dales straddle the border with Cumbria and are a mix of lush green valleys and wild, windswept moorland.

BRIGFLATTS The Quaker Friends Meeting House (below) at Brigflatts, half a mile from Sedbergh, was built in 1675. At this time, the village was a thriving community of around 75 people who ran their own cottage industry relying on flax weaving. In 1881 a raised wooden floor was fitted to allow water from the village pond to flow through the meeting house without wetting the feet of the congregation. The poet Basil Bunting (1900-1985) is buried in the Quaker graveyard in the village.

DENT The pretty village of Dent is actually in Cumbria, four miles south-east of Sedburgh, although it lies within the Yorkshire Dales National Park. The white-painted cottages are very Cumbrian in character in contrast to the warm natural stone buildings usually found in the lower Yorkshire Dales. Dent was once a centre of the knitting industry and the stockings and nightcaps produced by the villagers were sold widely across northern Yorkshire. The view (left) across the village looks towards High Hall on the lower slopes of Aye Gill Pike.

Malhamdale & Littondale

Busy Malhamdale is famous for its limestone scenery, while Littondale to the north remains a quiet, peaceful backwater.

Malhamdale is immensely popular because of its unique limestone landscape formed over millions of years, first by glacial erosion and then by the effects of wind, rain and frost. Three of the best examples – the limestone cliff at Malham Cove, Malham Tarn and Gordale Scar are sited behind the attractive village of Malham. Above the Cove lies Malham pavement (right) where hundreds of limestone blocks or "clints" are criss-crossed with deep fissures or "grykes".

MALHAM The attractive village of Malham (below) lies five miles west of Settle on the Pennine Way. The magnificent vertical limestone face of Malham Cove is three-quarters of a mile north of the village. Malham Tarn, England's highest freshwater lake, sits close to the limestone pavement at the top of the Cove. This lake was formed by glaciation during the last Ice Age. It was long thought that Malham Beck, which appears as if by magic at the base of Malham Cove and flows through the village, had Malham Tarn as its source. In fact the water from the tarn re-appears at Airehead Springs, south of the village.

ARNCLIFFE This pretty hamlet (right) lies at the heart of lovely Littondale and is the largest of its four settlements which also include the village of Litton and the small hamlets of Halton Gill and remote Foxup. Arncliffe has a central wide open green, surrounded by mellow stone cottages and farm buildings. Littondale was the setting for Charles Kingsley's *The Water Babies* and it was also chosen originally as the setting for the long-running television series *Emmerdale*. Several large porched barns indicate that this is still very much a typical Dales' working community. At the heart of the hamlet, close to the bridge over the river Skirfare, lies the pretty church of St Oswald's with its fine Victorian stained-glass windows.

HALTON GILL Situated at the northern end of Littondale and eight miles north-east of Settle, Halton Gill (right and below) has a most beautiful and quite spectacular setting. Surrounded and sheltered by Plover Hill, Cow Close Fell and Horse Head Moor, the village of Halton Gill sits comfortably beside the infant river Skirfare, which is fed by Cosh Beck, Foxup Beck and Hesleden Beck. The stone houses and farm buildings are mostly 17th century and one barn has a huge entrance porch dated 1829. In the photograph a flock of Swaledale sheep is shown being moved through the village whilst the photograph at the bottom shows fell runners crossing the packhorse bridge on Gala Day.

FOXUP This tiny hamlet (above) which consists of a number of working farms is the most remote of the settlements in Littondale and stands right at the top of the Dale. This viewpoint is from Low Bergh looking north over Foxup towards Ber Gill and Eller Carr Moss. Cosh Beck and Foxup Beck join just below the houses and run quickly downhill to form the river Skirfare just before Halton Gill.

HUBBERHOLME This tiny village (left), named after a Viking chieftain, is located on the Dales Way four and a half miles from Kettlewell and is famous for its beautiful church and atmospheric pub. Hubberholme is set at the foot of Langstrothdale, and consists of a cluster of old farm cottages surrounding the church and the George Inn. Hubberholme was a great favourite of the writer J B Priestley. Literary pilgrims visit the village to see the George Inn where he could often be found enjoying the local ale. Close by stands the church of St Michael and All Angels. The churchyard is the last resting place for Priestley's ashes. The choir stalls and the pews are much more recent and were made in 1934 by the renowned craftsman Robert Thompson, often known as the "Mouseman" of Kilburn because of the distinctive mouse carving with which he decorated his work.

Wharfedale & Nidderdale

The southerly dales of Wharfedale and Nidderdale have a wealth
of upland scenery dotted with attractive towns and villages.

KETTLEWELL In the shadow of Great Whernside 13 miles north of Skipton, Kettlewell is popular with potholers, climbers and walkers. Its buildings are clustered close to Cam Beck where it joins the river Wharfe. The Scarecrow Festival in Kettlewell (below) has become an increasingly popular community event, attracting ever more visitors to the village each year. The fields (left) lie just south of the village and were photographed from a footpath just above Crookacre Wood.

STARBOTTON Just two miles north of Kettlewell in Wharfedale, Starbotton was rebuilt during the latter part of the 17th century. Its close proximity to the river Wharfe meant it was almost completely swept away during the great flood of 1686. Starbotton lies deep within the national park. This photograph, left, was taken from the stony track that climbs up and out of the east side of the village, offering the serious walker an alternative route up to the summit of Buckden Pike, which at 2,302ft (701m) easily qualifies as a mountain. The settlement of Starbotton is first mentioned in the Domesday Book. Many of its cottages and barns date from the 17th century, when they were rebuilt. The local Fox and Hounds Inn in Starbotton is very popular with visitors after walking along the riverside or exploring the nearby fells. Along a rough road at the back of the village are the remains of a lead smelting mill.

KILNSEY The tiny village of Kilnsey (above) lies just three miles north of Grassington on the B6160 in the heart of Wharfedale. It nestles in the shadow of Kilnsey Crag, a dramatic peak much loved by climbers. Together with its glorious setting, Kilnsey has many attractions. These include the long-distance footpath, the Dales Way, which passes close by and pony-trekking from the village of Conistone just half a mile away across the valley. There is also fly-fishing and a nature trail at Kilnsey Park Trout Farm. The very popular Tennants Arms provides a warm and friendly welcome, typical of Dales' pubs. Kilnsey Crag towers high over the village – 170ft (52m) above the nearby B6160 – and is the most prominent landmark in Wharfedale. The 40ft (12m) overhang at the top provides an irresistible challenge to climbers and passing walkers are often to be seen gazing up in astonishment at their daring and agility. The Kilnsey Agricultural Show (below) is a showcase for the local farming community. Held every year on the Tuesday after the August Bank Holiday against the backdrop of Kilnsey Crag, it is the ideal opportunity for local people to get together and catch up on news and events.

GRASSINGTON The largest settlement in upper Wharfedale, Grassington has developed mainly due to its close proximity to the place where two historic roads cross in the dale. The village has many charming features including a cobbled square, the site of the farmers' market (right). At Christmas the shopkeepers in the village dress in Dickensian costume and transform Grassington into a Victorian village. After dark braziers are set up around the village square creating an authentic nineteenth-century atmosphere.

LINTON This characterful village of stone cottages is situated seven miles north of Skipton and one mile south of Grassington just off the B6160. It clusters around the large, irregular village green with the welcoming Fontaine Inn at its centre. The green slopes eastwards towards the grassy banks of Linton Beck. With its many elegant stone houses, Linton was voted the "prettiest village in the North" in 1949 and it appears that little has changed since then. An unusual building by the green, the Fontaine Hospital, was built in 1721 as almshouses for six poor men or women. Linton Beck is crossed by a packhorse bridge, a modern road bridge, a clapper bridge, stepping stones and fords. Just one mile from the village along the river Wharfe are waterfalls, a weir, riverside paths and the delightful St Michael's church.

APPLETREEWICK Four miles south-east of Grassington, this peaceful
Wharfedale village is situated on a steep slope with open views towards the
surrounding countryside. The main street is lined with ornate and characterful cottages and at either end there is Low Hall and High Hall. As can be seen
(above), Appletreewick nestles snugly on a south-facing slope above the river
Wharfe and is surrounded by some of the most beautiful scenery in
Wharfedale; to the right is the summit of Simon's Seat. This photograph was
taken from the slopes of Burnsall Fell. The distinctive Mock Beggar Hall
(right) in the centre of the village was built on the site of a grange used by the
monks of Bolton Priory. It is rumoured that one particularly wayward monk
was walled up inside the hall. Sir William Craven, Appletreewick's most
famous inhabitant, was known as "Dick Whittington of the Dales". A farmer's
son, he was sent to London to make his fortune and was so successful that
he became Lord Mayor of the City in 1610. Sir William rebuilt High Hall
and the building can be seen at the top of the hill.

BURNSALL Ten miles north-west of Ilkley, Burnsall is everything a Dales' village should be. Famous for its massive five-arched bridge, which spans the river Wharfe, it is one of the most photographed of all the Dales' villages. The shape of the village is very much dictated by the river. Many of the houses date back to the 17th century and are built from rich warm stone. The photograph of the village in the winter (above) was taken from Rowan Tree Crag shortly after sunrise in February. Every August Burnsall hosts England's oldest fell race (right), an event which is popular with both local people and visitors. There is a wonderful carnival atmosphere throughout the day, usually with a brass band playing. There are family races, and many other traditional community country sports on the green. A trip to the Dales would not be complete without visiting one of the many outstanding churches, and Wharfedale has its fair share. The parish church of St Wilfred is a fine example and is approached through a lych-gate. The Victorian stained-glass windows were donated by local parishioners, many of whom are buried in the churchyard.

BOLTON ABBEY The ruined Augustinian priory of Bolton Abbey (above) is situated close to Bolton Bridge, the "gateway" to Wharfedale. The abbey is popular with visitors, many of whom stay close to the monastic buildings, often choosing to picnic and spend the whole day by the river. Those who venture a little further along the splendid riverside walks will find some of Wharfedale's most popular attractions.

Two of the most spectacular are "the Strid", the narrow chasm through which the river Wharfe gushes in a thunderous cascade, and the enchanting Valley of Desolation with its waterfalls and wooded glades. Further upstream, along a nature trail, is Barden Bridge and the beautifully sited Barden Tower, built in 1485 by Lord Henry Clifford, and restored by Lady Anne Clifford in 1658. The photographs here of hoar frosts and spring bluebells illustrate this idyllic location through the seasons.

PATELEY BRIDGE The small town of Pateley Bridge (left and below) has many interesting nooks and crannies and should not be overlooked when travelling along the B6265 in upper Nidderdale. The town's narrow main street is dominated by elegant dark gritstone buildings but on either side there are pretty cobbled alleyways and passages which lead to hidden courtyards with a variety of cottages, galleries and craft shops. Over the centuries Pateley Bridge developed as both a market town for the local hill farmers and an industrial centre for textiles and leadmining. The townsfolk of Pateley Bridge take great pride in their spring and summer floral displays. The main street has a wide variety of interesting properties and shops including the oldest sweetshop in England, which dates from 1827. Open skies, panoramic views and narrow meandering lanes await the visitor on the steep slopes that surround this sheltered settlement.

MIDDLESMOOR Seven miles north-west of Pateley Bridge at the head of Nidderdale, Middlesmoor (above) clings to the top of a large hill, its stone cottages and cobbled streets huddled together to form a pretty and interesting hamlet. St Chad's church was restored in 1866 and its set of bells was donated by Mrs Barkwith in 1868. The old church was consecrated in 1484 in the reign of Richard III, by Drummond, Archbishop of York, at the request of the parishioners. The font is Anglo-Saxon which suggests that St Chad's was built on the site of an earlier church. The spectacular view of the Vale of Nidd from the churchyard (left and above right) is breathtaking.

Uredale

Less rugged than its upland neighbours, this green Dale contains a beautiful ruined abbey and some fine towns.

Once the river Ure leaves Wensleydale it continues towards Ripon, passing the beautiful abbey at Jervaulx and the villages of Masham and West Tanfield. Less rugged than many of the more traditional upland Dales, Uredale is a prosperous and attractive farming area. The city of Ripon with its historic cathedral and amenities is an ideal centre for visits to the southern and eastern Dales.

RIPON The gateway to the eastern Dales, Ripon is built around an attractive open square and boasts an elegant cathedral. This magnificent building overlooks the riverside houses on the banks of the Ure (left). A church was first established here over 1,300 years ago; the present building is the fourth to have occupied the site. The town has three unusual museums – the Courthouse, the Prison and Police Museum and the Workhouse Museum.

WEST TANFIELD Situated on the banks of the river Ure, the skyline of this attractive village (left) is dominated by the Marmion Tower and the church of St Nicholas. The tower is a 15th-century gatehouse noted for its great arch and window. Sir John and Lady Elizabeth Marmion, who owned the tower, are commemorated in a tomb (above) in the church.

JERVAULX ABBEY The beautiful ruins of Jervaulx Abbey (left) lie between Masham and Leyburn. The abbey was founded in 1156 by Cistercian monks who moved from Fors, higher up the valley, in search of better weather. The abbey was ruined after the Dissolution of the Monasteries in 1537; much of its fine stonework was looted and used in other local buildings. Despite its condition, enough remains of the ivy-covered crumbling walls to remind the visitor of the simple yet austere lives of the "white monks". A feature of the site today is the large number of wildflowers which adorn the ancient stones and surrounding parkland.

MASHAM Pronounced "massum" this is an attractive small town with a cobbled marketplace (left) which is surrounded by elegant Georgian houses, stone cottages, shops and tearooms. The spire of St Mary's overlooks the marketplace. The town is situated midway between Ripon and Leyburn on the western bank of the river Ure. Masham is home to two famous breweries: Theakston and the Black Sheep Brewery. The Masham Steam Engine and Fair Organ Rally (above) is a popular event every July.

Swaledale & Arkengarthdale

The elegant town of Richmond guards the approaches to these two northerly upland Dales.

Just off the B6270, Keld is situated in a very remote and attractive setting at the head of Swaledale, nine miles south-east of Kirby Stephen. The village name derives from the old Norse word for a spring. The stone houses of Keld (above) cluster around a chapel, and the village boasts its own literary institute. This photograph was taken from Swallow Hole just north of the village.

KELD ATTRACTIONS The hamlet (below) is the point at which the two long-distance footpaths, the Coast-to-Coast and the Pennine Way, intersect. The nearby river Swale is fed by many small becks which flow down from the fells. The attractive waterfall of East Gill Force (left) is 10 minutes' stroll from the village, just north of the Pennine Way, where the footpath crosses East Stonesdale. South-east of Keld, the prominent Kisdon Hill offers breathtaking views of the surrounding fells.

LANGTHWAITE The picturesque village of Langthwaite (left) is the largest settlement in Arkengarthdale, the most northerly of Yorkshire's dales. Its stone cottages huddle together haphazardly along Arkle Beck, three miles north-west of Reeth. The cosy Red Lion pub was used extensively in the filming of the television series *All Creatures Great and Small*. The "Waterloo" church of St Mary constructed in 1817 was typical of many churches built after the French Revolution to counteract atheism. During weddings in Langthwaite there is a local tradition of locking the church gates. Children then gather outside and the gates are only unlocked and the wedding party freed when money is tossed to them!

GUNNERSIDE The beautiful windswept fells and attractive patchwork of fields, drystone walls and barns along the valley bottom (above and top) make this part of Swaledale a favourite with visitors. In early summer the wildflower meadows are a vibrant sea of colour, and a delight to walk through. Gunnerside Gill runs through the tiny village of Gunnnerside and meets the Swale just below the King's Head Inn.

MUKER The pretty village of Muker (left) sits proudly above Straw Beck just before it joins the river Swale about one mile east of Thwaite. The church of St Mary the Virgin (right) dates from the reign of Elizabeth 1. The colourful east window of the church depicts the scenery around the village including the river Swale and Straw Beck, together with 23 horned sheep – a reference to Psalm 23, *The Lord is my Shepherd*. The view below is from the limestone mass of Kisdon Hill looking south towards the village with the river Swale meandering through the valley to the left.

RICHMOND The capital of Swaledale, Richmond (above and right) is dominated by its castle keep, part of the massive fortification built by Alan the Red of Brittany, a trusted supporter of William I. Richmond ranks among the most beautiful towns in England, with many elegant Georgian houses, cobbled streets and pretty cottage gardens. The town's prosperity grew with the wool trade and later the leadmining industry of Arkengarthdale. At the centre of the impressive marketplace is the 12th century chapel of the Holy Trinity, now used as the regimental museum of the Green Howards. In 1788, Samuel Butler, a local actor and manager, built the Theatre Royal, a beautiful Georgian theatre, which is still in use today. Situated in the middle of Richmond at the bottom of the marketplace and overlooked by Millgate House, a beautiful Georgian townhouse, is a pretty south-facing walled garden (left) open to the public between April and October.

REETH Situated 12 miles west of Richmond on the B6270, Reeth (left and above) was once a centre for both leadmining and knitting, and now continues to be the market town and focal point for the local community. The village of Reeth is an immensely popular tourist centre and one can easily see why. From its elevated position the spacious, triangular village green provides stunning views of the surrounding countryside. In Saxon times Reeth was a small settlement on the forest edge, but it later developed and grew so that by the time of the Norman Conquest its status warranted inclusion in the Domesday Book. August is the month for the Reeth agricultural show (right), a highlight of the farming year.

West Yorkshire

A mix of rugged moorland, attractive Pennine towns and major cities such as Leeds and Bradford.

West Yorkshire is a landscape of contrasts. There are great differences between the physical landscapes of the west and centre where the Pennines reach a height of 1,725ft (526m) and are cut into by the upper reaches of the valleys of the Wharfe, Aire and Calder and their tributaries – the rivers that made the region such an engine of growth and change during the Industrial Revolution – and the relatively low-lying eastern lowlands on the edge of the Vale of York. There are contrasts, too, in the urban landscapes of the great cities of Leeds and Bradford, the major towns of Halifax, Huddersfield and Wakefield, and small towns such as Keighley, Pontefract and Wetherby. But all is not urban and industrial: there are interesting and attractive villages such as Howarth and Heptonstall and a collection of great houses including Harewood, Temple Newsam and West Bretton set in landscaped parks.

CENTRAL LEEDS The commercial and financial capital of Yorkshire has many fine buildings. Dominating the heart of the city is Leeds Town Hall, constructed between 1853-58 and designed by Cuthbert Brodrick, the Hull architect. It is a solid and confident flagship of a proud Victorian city, topped by a magnificent domed clock-tower (left) rising to 225ft (68m). The owl is a symbol of Leeds that also appears on the city's coat of arms on Leeds Bridge (below). The three stars are from the coat of arms of the city's first mayor, Thomas Danby, the owls are from the coat of arms of the first alderman, Sir John Saville and the fleece, the sign of a wool stapler, reflects the importance of wool in the history of Leeds. The Victorian bridge was built between 1870-73.

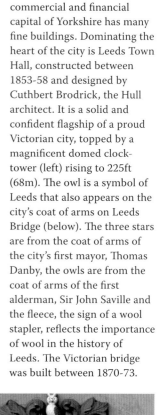

No 1 CITY SQUARE New building development is a hallmark of Leeds. No 1 City Square was completed in 1998, a 12-storey block with a black granite base, white limestone upper storeys and external lift shaft. Leeds Waterfront (far left) was the city's dockland area at the termini of the Aire and Calder Navigation and the Leeds and Liverpool Canal. By the 1960s this area was partially derelict. It has now been transformed: many of the warehouses have been converted and smart new apartment blocks constructed.

RETAIL QUARTER

Leeds is a bustling retail, commercial and financial centre. The treasures of the retail quarter are the covered shopping arcades: Thornton's Arcade (1877-8), Grand Arcade (1897), Queen's Arcade (1899) and County Arcade (1898-1904). The County Arcade (above) presents the visitor with one of the most beautiful shopping environments in the city. It is 394ft (120m) long and has mahogany shopfronts with curved glass windows, separated by pilasters and columns of Siena marble above which are balustraded balconies crowned by an arched cast-iron roof. St Peter's (left), Leeds parish church, standing in Kirkgate was built between 1837-41 to replace the medieval church. Its tall tower, topped by battlements and pinnacles, is a Leeds landmark. The church does not stand in a central position in the city: it had to be constructed slightly away from the centre due to the building of the railway embankment to the north in the 19th century.

PARK ROW
HOUSE

KIRKSTALL ABBEY The ruins of Kirkstall Abbey (right) lie just three miles north-west of the city centre. The abbey was founded in 1147 by monks and lay brothers from Fountains Abbey. In 1890 the site was bought from a private owner and presented to Leeds Corporation who opened it as a public park in 1893.

OXFORD PLACE Oxford Chambers (left) stands in Oxford Place, close to the Town Hall. It is attached to, and in the same style as, the Methodist Church next door and is typical of many of the fine late Victorian and early Edwardian buildings still to be found in the city.

ROUNDHAY PARK This 373-acre public park, the largest in Leeds, was opened in 1872. It was first mentioned in the 12th century when it was a deer park owned by the de Lacy family and part of the boundary ditch still survives in the north-east corner. The park was bought in 1871 by the Lord Mayor of Leeds and a group of associates who then sold it to the Corporation. It was slow to develop as a popular attraction and was nicknamed "The Great White Elephant" until the electric trams reached it in the early 1890s. Among its attractions are the 33-acre Waterloo Lake which is fed from the north by a series of cascades and waterfalls, the smaller Upper Lake, a sham castle, the Canal Gardens, the Alhambra Garden, Monet Garden and the Coronation House (now Tropical World).

HAREWOOD HOUSE This magnificent country house (above), the home of Earl and Countess Lascelles, was built by the York architect John Carr between 1759 and 1772 on the instructions of Edwin Lascelles whose father had made his fortune in the ribbon trade, from his position as collector of customs in Barbados and his directorship of the East India Company. The interiors were the work of Robert Adam and much of the furniture is by Thomas Chippendale. In the 1840s the south façade of the house was remodelled by Sir Charles Barry, the architect of the Houses of Parliament. The grounds were laid out by Lancelot "Capability" Brown. To the south of the house is an ornamental garden with intricate flowerbeds, fountains and herbaceous borders.

PONTEFRACT The beautiful octagonal tower of St Giles' church (left) stands sentry over Pontefract, and is visible for miles around. St Giles mainly dates from the Georgian era, but the site has been a centre of religious worship since the 12th century. The church interior contains splendid stained-glass windows some of which are dedicated to long-serving vicars and prominent Pontefract families. Between 1868-9, the Earl of Harewood built the beautiful Sanctuary Chapel. Overlooking the market square stands the Buttercross. It was gifted to the town by Solomon Dupier who vowed to erect a covered market cross if his wife and three daughters survived the smallpox they had all contracted. In the event they did recover but all four lost their sight; nevertheless, in 1734 the Buttercross was built and provided shelter for the country women who brought their dairy produce to market well into the 20th century.

WAKEFIELD An inland port on the river Calder, Wakefield's prosperity stemmed from the wool trade. The Cathedral of All Saints (left) has a fine musical tradition and boasts Yorkshire's tallest spire at 247ft (75m). The old Wakefield toll bridge is home to the medieval St Mary's Chantry chapel, one of only six bridge chapels built in Britain. Today Wakefield is famous for the Yorkshire Sculpture Park (bottom) at Bretton Hall. Set within beautiful parkland, thousands of visitors come each year to be inspired by exhibits of modern and contemporary sculpture in a superb natural setting. The collection includes works by Henry Moore, Barbara Hepworth and Eduardo Paolozzi.

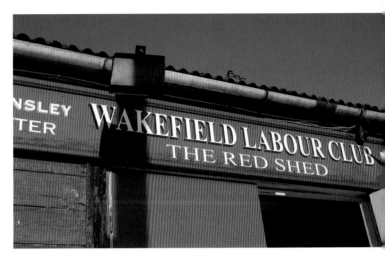

CLIFFE CASTLE MUSEUM, KEIGHLEY Set amidst beautiful parkland, the mansion at Keighley (right) is not a medieval castle but a Victorian one – created by the textile magnate Henry Isaac Butterfield who transformed the earlier Cliffe Hall into the enchanting Cliffe Castle in 1878. In 1950 Sir Bracewell Smith, a local man, bought the castle and presented it to the people as a museum; today it is a treasure trove of natural history and geology, local artefacts, furniture and stained glass – including a set of William Morris panels made for the Temple Street Methodist Chapel in Keighley in 1921.

COW AND CALF Up on the famous Ilkley Moor, two rocky outcrops of millstone grit (below) have long been known as the Cow and Calf rocks; with their steep slopes these and other outcrops are popular with climbers of all abilities. Ilkley Moor is part of Rombalds Moor which rises to over 1,600ft (396m) in places. It is rich in archaeological remains including cairns, barrows, hut circles and "cup and ring" carvings. The moor has long been a favourite with walkers – from the top there are glorious views over Wharfedale.

BRADFORD The Alhambra Theatre (above) was built in 1914 for the musical impressario Frank Laidler, the "King of Pantomime". It was restored in 1986 after suggestions that it might be demolished and a car park built in its place. The magnificent neo-Gothic Town Hall (right) dates from 1873; the scale of the building reflects Bradford's prominence and its ambition as a commercial centre of trade, worthy of being ranked with other cities such as Liverpool and Glasgow. Re-named City Hall in 1965, its frontage overlooks Centenary Square and is graced with sculptures of British monarchs and Oliver Cromwell – an echo of Bradford's role in the Civil War. Two of Bradford's surviving medieval buildings are Bolling Hall and the Cathedral. Now a museum, and just a mile from the city centre, Bolling Hall gives visitors an insight into the lives and times of the two families for whom it provided a home over five hundred years.

FIVE RISE LOCKS

The engineers who built Britain's canals in the early days of the Industrial Revolution had to overcome many challenges, including the differing levels of the countryside through which they drove this new mode of transport. Completed in 1777, Five Rise Locks at Bingley on the Leeds and Liverpool Canal raises the level of the waterway by 59ft (18m). On the Yorkshire side of the Pennines, as the canal rises out of Airedale, there are, within a 16-mile stretch, three double locks, four staircase locks of three locks each, and then the Bingley Rise – originally called the Bingley Great Lock.

HAWORTH The photograph below left is of the Brontë Parsonage Museum at Haworth; the one below is of the town centre. When the Rev Patrick Brontë brought his family to live at the parsonage in Haworth in 1820 the village was little more than a cluster of stone cottages clinging to a steep hill, with the church at the top of the street and the moors stretching into the distance. Today the fame of this extraordinary family has spread far and wide and visitors descend on the town and the museum in their thousands. The Parsonage is full of paintings, books and papers that belonged to the Brontës and the rooms have been lovingly restored to convey to visitors what life was like for the parson and his family of writers. The village retains its Victorian air with cobbled streets, and a collection of old-fashioned shops.

HALIFAX Built in a valley seven miles south-west of Bradford, Halifax is the capital of Calderdale. The town owes its prosperity to the wool trade and its town hall was designed by Sir Charles Barry, the architect of the Houses of Parliament. The Piece Hall, completed in 1779, contains more than 300 rooms built around an open quadrangle; it was here that handloom weavers living in outlying cottages bought their "pieces" of woollen cloth to sell. The Wainhouse Tower (right) was built for John Edward Wainhouse to carry the smoke and fumes produced by his dye works out of the Calder valley. At 253ft (77m) high it is one of Calderdale's best-loved landmarks. The beautiful Victoria Theatre (above) was built in 1901 originally as a concert hall. It was converted into a theatre in 1960 and the interior has recently been extensively restored.

HEBDEN BRIDGE AND HEPTONSTALL Eight miles west of Halifax, the beautiful town of Hebden Bridge grew rapidly in the 18th and 19th centuries as a result of the wool trade, the fast-flowing waters of the river Calder providing power for the mills in the area. The wool trade brought the Rochdale Canal (above), completed in 1804; this canal is particularly popular as its route crosses the Pennines, giving wonderful views of the breathtaking scenery of Calderdale. The original settlement of Hebden Bridge centred on the hilltop village of Heptonstall; the magnificent view (left) is of Hebden Bridge from Heptonstall. Heptonstall is home to two churches, which both share the same graveyard. The ruined church of St Thomas a Becket (below) dates from 1256.

HUDDERSFIELD The West Riding town of Huddersfield boasts 1,660 listed buildings – only Bristol and Westminster have more. One of the town's most famous sons was the Labour prime minister Harold Wilson. His statue (above) was erected in 1999 and graces St George's Square in front of the railway station. The magnificent town hall (right) doubles as a concert hall and is home to the renowned Huddersfield Choral Society. It was designed by John H Abbey and built between 1875 and 1881. It is "classic Italianate" in style, defined by the rounded heads to the windows and the symmetrical design. The inset photograph shows a decoration on one of the cast iron pillars supporting the roof of the open air market.

HOLME VALLEY The Digley reservoir (left) is one of a number in the upper Holme valley overlooking Holmfirth. Immediately to the west is the smaller Bilberry reservoir which burst its banks in 1852, causing the death of 81 people in the valley below.

CASTLE HILL The hill fort at Almondbury near Huddersfield, seen below from Farnley Tyas, is made up of a series of Iron Age and medieval earthworks. The flat-topped hill has been the site of Chartist rallies as well as prize-fighting. The Victoria or Jubilee tower was added in 1899 to celebrate Queen Victoria's Diamond Jubilee two years earlier.

HOLMFIRTH Three miles south of Huddersfield, Holmfirth is situated at the confluence of the rivers Holme and Ribble. This picturesque Pennine town developed rapidly in the 16th century thanks to the cloth industry and its slate and stone mines. Now the town and its surrounding countryside are famous as the setting for the long-running television series *Last of the Summer Wine*. Thousands of tourists flock to the area each year to enjoy the scenery and hoping to identify locations used in the series. Sid's Café (above left) in the centre of the town, a watering hole familiar to all *Last of the Summer Wine* viewers, is now a place of pilgrimage for fans. Next door to the character Nora Batty's fictional house is the Summer Wine exhibition (left) which combines the Wrinkled Stocking Tea Room and a re-creation of the character Compo's home.

North York Moors

A captivating landscape of heather moorland and remote valleys with characterful villages and market towns.

One of the finest upland landscapes in Britain, the North York Moors include the north-east corner of Yorkshire stretching northwards from the Vale of Pickering to the border with County Durham and from the Hambleton and Cleveland Hills in the west to the coast. A large part of the region has been designated as a national park. With its heather-clad moorland, fertile dales and characterful villages and market towns, this region has one of Yorkshire's most beautiful and captivating landscapes. Dales penetrate the moorlands; from the North Sea coast, for example, Eskdale runs deep inland and Farndale and Rosedale penetrate northwards from the Vale of Pickering. These dales within the moorlands have always been very important. They have heavy clay soils that are variable in quality, but in such barren surroundings they play a crucial role and contain almost all the village settlements.

MALLYAN SPOUT The highest waterfall on the North York Moors, Mallyan Spout (right) near Goathland, cascades 60ft (18m) down the side of Beck Gorge. A short walk alongside the beck just to the right of the Mallyan Spout Hotel leads to the waterfall. In wet and windy weather, spray is blown across the path giving visitors the impression of walking through the waterfall itself.

LITTLEBECK The tiny hamlet of Littlebeck (below) which derives its name from Little Beck, a tributary of the river Esk, lies hidden away in a deep secluded valley on the edge of Littlebeck Wood. The roads surrounding the village have names such as Goathland Banks, Lousy Hill and Blue Bank, all of which convey the steeply-sided nature of the approach. Reaching the village is quite tricky as the roads are narrow and caution is recommended. At the bottom of the valley there is a tiny chapel and a ford across Little Beck.

GOATHLAND This pretty village is immensely popular with visitors who are drawn to it because of its *Heartbeat* associations – in the television series the village is Aidensfield and many of the landmarks shown in the programmes, including the railway station, can be easily identified on a short walk around the village. The station also appears as Hogsmeade station in the *Harry Potter* films.

GLAISDALE Nestling in the Esk Valley, the village of Glaisdale is a past "Village of the Year" winner for the North of England. The valley around Glaisdale is a majestic sight when viewed in winter from high on the fellside (above left). The photograph was taken from the roadside near Low Gill Beck Farm, looking towards Glaisdale Moor. The area once had an abundance of iron ore and in the mid 19th century three blast furnaces were built there.

FRYUP DALE This quaintly-named corner of North Yorkshire consists of two secluded valleys, Great and Little Fryup, made up of a scattering of farms and cottages. Winding off the Esk Valley the area is totally unspoilt and surrounded by magnificent purple heather-clad moors with trails and walks across the moorland. Fryup Dale (left) is an ideal place from which to explore *Heartbeat* country, either on foot or by bike.

ROSEDALE This long, extended valley (above) stretches out in a south-easterly direction from Westerdale Moor and Danby High Moor towards Hartoft End and Cropton Forest. The river Seven flows throughout its length gathering water from the numerous moorland springs and streams. The rail-bed of the disused Rosedale Mineral Railway is clearly visible around the perimeter of the dale and stunning views of the valley can be enjoyed from many of the moorland paths and in particular from Chimney Bank Top.

ROSEDALE ABBEY
Although this delightful village is called Rosedale Abbey it has never had an abbey, but instead was the site of a small Cistercian nunnery. Today, only a stone turret remains. The parish church of St Lawrence (left) is at the heart of the village. The Rosedale Show takes place every August.

LEVISHAM This picturesque village is an attractive stop on the North York Moors Railway. The village nestles above the quiet and winding wooded valley of Newton Dale, seven miles north of Pickering. Its village green is unusually wide and is lined with characterful stone cottages and farm buildings. The small church of St John the Baptist (below) lies at the top of the village where the road and a footpath, which meanders across woods and fields, leads to the railway station in the bottom of the valley. Levisham station is set in the secluded and scenic Newton Dale Valley. The station has been used as a location in a number of television programmes including *All Creatures Great and Small*, *Poirot*, *Sherlock Holmes* and *Brideshead Revisited*.

CROPTON The little village of Cropton (left) nestles on the southern edge of Cropton Forest, between Helmsley and Pickering. At the top of the village main street stands Cropton village well, a reminder of a bygone era. The well (left) was restored in 1988 when the remains of the winding gear were found nearby. To the east of the village lies St Gregory's church which has a 10th-century cross in its graveyard. The New Inn at Cropton is 200 years old and is at the heart of village life. In 1984 the Cropton Brewery was established in its cellars, reviving a centuries-old tradition of brewing in the village. Cropton Ales are well regarded, and include the Pullman Pint, a real ale which is named after the North Yorkshire Moors Railway.

PICKERING The elegant market town of Pickering (right) is located on the southern edge of the North York Moors. It dates from the 3rd century BC, and has a motte-and-bailey castle with Norman remnants. In the centre of the town is Beck Isle Museum of Rural Life. The museum has 27 galleries and visitors are transported back through time as they pass through a wide variety of recreated settings including a cobblers' shop, blacksmiths, chemists' shop, dairy and village store. One gallery features the work of local photographer Sydney Smith who captured the atmosphere of rural life in and around Pickering in the late 19th and early 20th centuries. His work ranks alongside that of Frank Meadow Sutcliffe of Whitby.

CASTLETON Situated in the upper Esk Valley, the village of Castleton (below) sits proudly on a high ridge, where the lush green secluded valleys of Westerdale and Danby Dale come together. The settlement is steeped in history. The village hall, built in 1869, was called the Temperance Hall until 15 years ago – a throwback to the days when Temperance Societies, aiming to discourage the consumption of alcohol, existed in nearly every settlement. The village has a Quaker graveyard with gravestones dating from 1815 to 1944. Remains of the old castle, built by Robert De Brus, are now part of a house. Most of the castle was dismantled in 1216, and around 1240 some of the stones were used to restore Danby Church.

WESTERDALE The monument named Young Ralph Cross (right) stands next to the symbol marking the geological centre of the North York Moors; in 1974 it was adopted as the emblem of the national park. The cross was erected in the 18th century where an earlier named cross, Crux Radulph, once stood. Today the cross marks the point where the minor road into Westerdale joins the Hutton Le Hole to Castleton road at Rosedale Head. Records of the cross go as far back as 1200 and in 1550 it was constructed of wood. It is said that the present cross was erected in memory of a destitute traveller who died from exhaustion. A Danby farmer called Ralph discovered him and later decided to erect a cross where he found the body. There is clear evidence on the moor above Dale View in Westerdale (left) that the area has been inhabited since at least the Bronze Age. At Cairnfield around one hundred individual cairns and traces of metal workings have been discovered including an axe-hammer and other prehistoric remains.

BILSDALE & BLAKEY RIDGE Fangdale Beck village (above) lies between Bilsdale West Moor and Bilsdale East Moor. There are many excellent walks over the moors from this sleepy hamlet. Bilsdale has one of the oldest buildings on the North Yorks Moors – the Old Sun Inn, built in 1550. It has been used as both a farm-worker's cottage and shoemaker's workshop. It was opened as a licensed inn in 1774 and closed in 1914 when the Sun Inn was built across the yard. A short distance to the east lies the world famous coast-to-coast trail from St Bees in Cumbria to Robin Hood's Bay. Another long-distance path crosses close by – the 41-mile Lyke Wake Walk – which takes you past Bronze Age burial mounds and stone markers.

FARNDALE The tiny and picturesque hamlet of Church Houses (right) nestles between the mighty Rudland Rigg and Blakey Ridge in glorious scenery at the heart of this much-loved dale. Perhaps best known for its wild daffodils in spring, Farndale attracts up to 40,000 visitors each April. The daffodil walk begins in the village of Low Mill and follows the valley bottom beside the river Dove, all the way to Church Houses and its welcoming pub, the Feversham Arms Inn. In 1995 most of Farndale was designated a Local Nature Reserve in order to protect the daffodils.

GILLAMOOR The pretty village of Gillamoor lies 2.5 miles north of Kirby Moorside on the minor road that links Fadmoor to Hutton Le Hole. The village is famously known for its Surprise View at the eastern end of the hamlet, beside St Aidan's Church (below). The view of lower Farndale from this point is captivating and memorable whatever the season. The tiny church was rebuilt singlehandedly by James Smith of Farndale in 1802. At the centre of Gillamoor is the

Royal Oak, a listed building and characterful pub. In the photograph below, early morning winter mist slowly drifts northwards along the bottom of Douthwaite Dale looking to the north-west from Gillamoor. In spring, the banks around this area are festooned in a sea of wild-flowers. From here, there are footpaths leading from the village into the valley and up over the moors. A wide variety of birds can be seen in the area, including lapwings, curlews, snipe, fieldfares and finches.

RIEVAULX ABBEY Traditionally Cistercian abbeys were built on an east-west axis, but because of the steep slope at Rievaulx a north-south alignment was adopted. Like all Cistercian houses the location was deliberately secluded from the outside world and this particular site in the depths of the narrow river Rye valley must have provided the monks and lay brethren with a haven of peace and solitude. The 13th-century church (above) is reputed to have been one of the finest monastic churches in northern Britain and thankfully remains substantially intact. The abbey site is now owned and run by English Heritage, whereas Rievaulx Terrace and Temples (below), situated on an escarpment above the abbey, is owned by the National Trust. From this position it is possible to enjoy wonderful views of the abbey and surrounding countryside.

HELMSLEY This is one of the prettiest country towns in North Yorkshire. Located on the Thirsk to Scarborough road, Helmsley is a popular destination and an ideal centre for touring the local area. The market square is surrounded by a variety of gift shops, pubs, restaurants and galleries and on most weekends there is a lively atmosphere. A stream runs through the town at the back of the market square (right) complete with stone arch bridge; a resident large flock of white ducks are often to be seen waddling up and down. William Wordsworth stayed at the Black Swan Inn in the centre of the town when courting Mary, his future wife. Helmsley

Castle is a spectacular ruin and once guarded the Rye Valley. The early 13th-century castle is surrounded by a formidable double ditch cut from solid rock. Sir Charles Duncombe purchased the castle after it was rendered useless by Oliver Cromwell and it has subsequently been owned by the Earls of Feversham who are descended from Sir Charles. The Feversham family live in the Vanbrugh-built mansion in nearby Duncombe Park on the edge of the village.

HAWNBY The remote village of Hawnby lies in the Hambleton Hills in Upper Ryedale just north-west of Riveaulx. It is a village of two halves, which are split by a steep hill. The church of All Saints (right) is isolated and some distance from the village. Historical sources record that in the middle of the 18th century two men, Chapman and Cornforth, experienced vivid dreams of God speaking to them. They subsequently met the preacher John Wesley and were inspired to become the first Methodists in the neighbourhood. Unfortunately their homes at the top of the hill were owned by Lord Tancred who was an Anglican and very much opposed to their cause. They were expelled from Hawnby and resettled in the valley by the bridge, and so the village developed in two separate parts.

OLD BYLAND The tiny hamlet of Old Byland (right) is located just west of Rievaulx Abbey in the south-west corner of the North Yorks Moors. The village consists of a few stone cottages and farm buildings surrounding a small village green. The church of All Saints (left) is steeped in history and there has been a church of one kind or another on this site since Saxon times. Following the Norman Conquest the area was ravaged by William the Conqueror's army. The Domesday Book records for 1086 state that only two settlements, Helmsley and Old Byland, survived and that there was "a priest and a wooden church" in the village.

SUTTON BANK Views from Sutton Bank (below) over the Vale of York and Mowbray towards the Yorkshire Dales are deservedly considered to be some of the finest in the north of England. The Hambleton Escarpment rises abruptly to a height of around 1,000ft (300m) and you can often see for more than 30 miles. Roulston Scar and Hood Hill to the left are bathed in warm evening light as the sun sets over the dales far away to the west and Gormire Lake to the right is silhouetted by a dramatic sky.

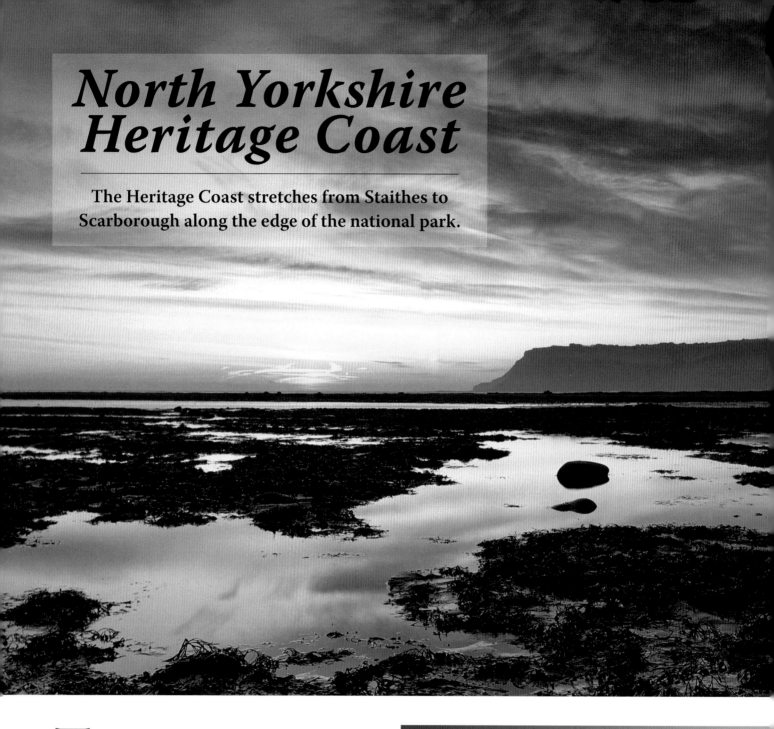

North Yorkshire Heritage Coast

The Heritage Coast stretches from Staithes to Scarborough along the edge of the national park.

The Yorkshire coast stretches from the county border at Staithes, just a few kilometres south of the river Tees in Cleveland, to Spurn Point, a long sandy promontory located on the south-eastern tip of the Holderness plain, on the northern bank of the Humber estuary. This beautiful and varied landscape is unique with high rugged cliffs, traditional fishing villages, small river inlets and wide sandy bays. The eastern coastal section of the North Yorks Moors national park is known as the Heritage Coast. The larger fishing towns of Whitby, Scarborough, Bridlington and Filey are steeped in history and charm – so much so that holidaymakers, artists, poets and photographers return again and again, to enjoy this stunningly beautiful region.

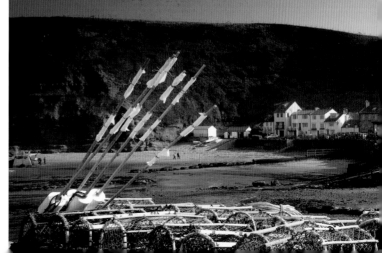

RUNSWICK'S COBLES This pretty village lies about 5 miles north of Whitby. Just above the sandy beach is the boat park (left) with its many *cobles* – small wooden fishing boats, a favourite subject for artists and photographers. The village has a tiny Methodist chapel, an Institute – a local meeting place which was opened in 1870 – an old lifeboat house and a former coastguard house with a thatched roof. Runswick has suffered many times from the ravages of the North Sea and in 1682 a landslide destroyed the entire village with the exception of one cottage. Thankfully no one was hurt as the locals were alerted by two mourners attending a wake, who realised what was about to happen. In 1970 sea wall defences were completed so the settlement is not as vulnerable as previously.

KETTLENESS Kettleness can be reached on foot through the hamlet of Goldsborough, which is just west of Lythe on the A174 coast road. There are many headlands on the North Yorkshire coast with the name "ness" or "nose". The cliffs at Kettleness (right) are deeply scarred by massive landslips and old alum mines. There was a huge landslip in the 19th century, when several clifftop houses were swept down onto the beach. Fortunately this happened on Sunday evening when the inhabitants were all attending the local Methodist Chapel.

STAITHES Known colloquially as "Steers", meaning "landing place", Staithes (left) is in a dramatic setting. Over the years, storms have taken their toll on the village and some landmarks, such as the original Cod and Lobster pub, and Captain Cook's old shop and home have long since been washed into the sea. The young James Cook received his first taste of the sea and ships at Staithes. In the late 1890s the so-called Staithes Group of around 30 artists were active in the area, developing the best in British Impressionist painting. Many examples of their work, including paintings by Dame Laura Knight and Joseph Bagshawe, are in major public collections, including Tate Britain in London.

SANDSEND This pretty fishing village (above) is located at the foot of Lythe Bank where the sandy beach that begins at Whitby, just two miles to the south, comes to an abrupt end. There are many picturesque stone cottages set against a backdrop of cliffs and beside two meandering streams which flow out onto the long sandy beach. Local walks follow the trackbed of the disused coastal railway and close by is the earthworks of Mulgrave Castle hidden away in Mulgrave Woods, just inland. Sandsend was important for the mining of alum and the massive waste piles on Sandsend Ness show the results of more than 250 years of quarrying.

WHITBY Often referred to as Captain Cook's Country, the seaside town of Whitby and the surrounding countryside, from where the young James Cook drew inspiration and learned the seafarer's trade, is steeped in maritime history. Cook was born in Marton, a small village just south of Middlesbrough. His first job was in Staithes, where he assisted the merchant William Sanderson. In 1746 he took up residence in John Walker's house, an elegant 17th-century harbourside house in Grape Lane, where he served his apprenticeship and learned about navigation and seamanship. The house is now the splendid Captain Cook Memorial Museum with a fine collection of original exhibits about the life of Yorkshire's most famous son. The author Bram Stoker (1847-1912) set much of his classic Victorian novel *Dracula* in and around the town and today visitors with a taste for the gothic can retrace the steps of the "undead" by taking the Dracula Trail Tour. The photographer Frank Meadow Sutcliffe (1853-1941) is Whitby's most famous artist. He immortalised the town and the life of its fishing community in scores of beautiful, sepia-tinted photographs, many of which can be seen at the Sutcliffe Gallery. Whitby's skyline is dominated by the ruins of St Hilda's Abbey, high up on East Cliff. Just nearby is the parish church of St Mary.

SALTWICK BAY The steep cliffs at Saltwick Bay, about one mile south-east of Whitby, are constantly being eroded by the wind and sea. Access to the bay is via a steep winding path that leads down to its soft sandy centre. On either side of the beach are vast rock platforms which are revealed as the tide recedes. Black Nab (above) is a distinctive rocky outcrop which sits in a solitary position in the centre of the beach. In the foreground lies the wreck of the fishing vessel *Admiral Von Tromp* which was trapped in 1976 on nearby rocks by heavy seas and fog with the loss of two of its crew.

ROBIN HOOD'S BAY The picturesque fishing village of Robin Hood's Bay (left and right) is one of the highlights of the Yorkshire coast. Its steep winding streets and cobbled ginnels (narrow alleyways between the buildings) are lined with old houses and cottages, many with red pantiled roofs, and everywhere there is the sound of the gulls which nest on the rooftops and chimneystacks. Legend has it that Robin Hood once repelled Danish invaders here; during the 18th century, goods were smuggled ashore by means of secret tunnels below the houses. The 190-mile Coast to Coast long-distance footpath ends at Robin Hood's Bay.

RAVENSCAR Located 183m (600ft) above sea level, Ravenscar is one of the wildest and most exposed places in Yorkshire. The winds that blow across the North Sea sweep down from the Arctic Ocean, so it's no surprise that the once planned town (a resort to rival nearby Scarborough) fell into difficulties and was not finally developed here. Today the 18th-century Raven Hall at the top of the cliff is a hotel situated on the site of a Roman signal point. The headland is now owned by the National Trust. There are fabulous views of the sweeping Robin Hood's Bay from the coastal clifftop path (above). The long-distance footpath, the Cleveland Way, leads north to Robin Hood's Bay and south to Ravenscar, offering ramblers and holidaymakers an abundance of spectacular views of the sea along this section, and ornithologists are often afforded close sightings of a large variety of seabirds.

The Holiday Coast

Resorts such as Scarborough, Bridlington and Filey make this stretch of coast a firm favourite with holidaymakers.

Developed as Britain's first seaside resort, Scarborough is one of the north of England's most popular coastal towns. Anne Brontë died in Scarborough at the young age of 28. She had been seriously ill with consumption and visited the resort with her sister, Charlotte, in the hope that the sea air would cure her condition. She is buried in the graveyard of St Mary's church. Founded just over a thousand years ago Scarborough is, historically, a relatively young settlement. Its name is derived from that of Thorgils Skarthi, the Viking raider who settled on this rocky and wild headland. The lighthouse, a harbour beacon, built in 1806 on the end of Vincent's Pier, was all but destroyed by an enemy raid on December 16 1914. The town is divided into two bays, North Bay and South Bay, by a huge headland and castle. The photograph above is of sunrise at South Bay, looking towards Filey.

FILEY A beautiful seaside town, Charlotte Brontë once stayed at Cliff House, and other famous visitors include the composer Frederic Delius and the Mountbatten family. The five-mile sandy beach is protected from the north by the magnificent Filey Brigg. The town's attractions include the Coble Landing, where fishing boats rest at jaunty angles. There is an Edwardian festival every year, when strawberry teas are served by ladies in period costume. Brass bands, barrel organs and the traditional Punch and Judy show provide fun for all ages.

SCARBOROUGH Perched on a rocky headland, the ruined Scarborough Castle (above and below) dominates the skyline. On a clear day a fantastic view can be enjoyed from the site, which is now in the care of English Heritage. One of the town's main attractions is the Spa Complex with its superb parks, gardens, theatres and conference hall which sits majestically beside the main bathing beach. Although the harbour is now chiefly used by leisure cruisers and yachts, fish is still landed here. Scarborough became a major fishing port after King Henry II built the castle in the 1170s and this led to the development of the famous Scarborough Fair, a six-week trading festival, which attracted merchants from all over Europe. In the first few decades of the 20th century it was not uncommon to see barrels of fish packed in salt lining Vincent's Pier, before being transported to inland markets for sale.

BEMPTON CLIFFS At 400ft (122m) Bempton (right) has some of the highest cliffs on the east coast of Britain, and is famous as a seabird nature reserve, featuring the only gannet colony in mainland Britain. Situated just north of Flamborough Head and close to Bridlington, access for visitors is easy by car or on foot, from the little village of Bempton one mile inland. The cliffs stretch for approximately six miles from Flamborough Head north towards Filey and at some points are more than 100m high. The hard chalk from which they are composed gives nesting birds many sheltered headlands and crevices, which are ideal for breeding. The RSPB bought the cliffs in 1969 and created one of the best places on the east coast to observe seabirds. A highlight of the reserve is its gannet colony (below), which can be seen at Bempton between January and November; the birds are most active between April and August when they are breeding. The gannet is Britain's largest seabird, and the number nesting at Bempton Cliffs has increased in recent years. In 1969 there were just 21 gannets' nests compared to 3,940 in 2005. Other birds in the reserve include razorbills, kittiwakes and the Atlantic puffin. These attractive birds, with their waddling gait and brightly coloured clown-like faces, are best seen between April and July. The

historic village of Bempton lies four miles north of Bridlington. With its stone cottages, guesthouses and the quaint White Horse Inn, the village is the ideal starting point for a clifftop walk.

FLAMBOROUGH To the east of Bempton, Flamborough Head juts eight miles out into the sea to the north of Bridlington. This dramatic promontory combines stunning white cliffs with picturesque sheltered shingle coves swept by the sea. Thornwick Bay (below) is just one of the many coves which make up the headland. The cliffs and coves teem with seabirds. Two lighthouses are sited on the headland. The first, a chalk tower, was built in 1669 by Sir John Clayton, but it was never kindled. It is the oldest surviving complete lighthouse in England. The lighthouse (right) was built by John Matson of Bridlington in 1806 at a cost of £8,000 and is still in use. It was automated in 1996 and guards the approaches to the busy shipping lanes that serve the ports of Scarborough and Bridlington.

SEWERBY Situated on the cliffs overlooking Bridlington Bay, this attractive village lies two miles north of Bridlington. The magnificent Sewerby Hall is a Grade 1 listed building set in 50 acres of landscaped gardens. The house was built between 1714 and 1720 by John Greame. The rooms on the ground floor are in Georgian, Regency and Victorian styles. Today the Orangery and Swinton rooms and their wonderful settings are used for civil marriage ceremonies, piano recitals, concerts, seminars, art workshops and many other activities. On other floors in the house there are exhibitions, galleries and a heritage library. The park and gardens (left) are teeming with attractions including a zoo, woodland walks, formal gardens and picnic areas. The beach at Sewerby (right), with Bridlington in the distance, marks the point where the white cliffs of Flamborough Head descend slowly towards the sandy beach at Bridlington.

BRIDLINGTON With its two glorious long sandy beaches, miles of elegant promenades, a very pretty and bustling harbour, as well as shops, amusements, restaurants and cafés, Bridlington has all the essential ingredients for the perfect family holiday. Flamborough Head and the lighthouse are clearly visible from the north pier and beach. The town is divided into two parts: the historic market town, approximately one mile inland, which grew up around the abbey of Bridlington Priory, and the fishing port of Bridlington Quay which developed as a holiday resort in Victorian times with the arrival of the railway in 1846. In recent years the large fleet of trawlers has diminished and now the harbour (left and above) buzzes with the sound of yachts and pleasure craft.

HORNSEA This small seaside resort is situated 16 miles north of Hull and 14 miles south of Bridlington. The historic town centre dates back to the 15th century. Hornsea is well known for its famous pottery which was first set up in 1949. There is also a folk museum which was established in 1978, and is housed in an 18th-century farmhouse. Perhaps Hornsea's best known attraction is its Mere. Surprisingly the Mere is the largest freshwater lake in Yorkshire. It covers 467 acres, compared to Semerwater in the Yorkshire Dales which covers 80 acres. Formed by glacial deposits at the end of the last ice age it is one of many water-filled hollows, a reminder that the area once resembled the Norfolk Broads. Due to the Mere's close proximity to the North Sea it attracts

a wide variety of over-wintering birds, including tufted ducks, goldeneyes and gadwalls. Activities on the Mere for both visitors and locals include rowing, sailing, boat trips and fishing. The parish church of St Nicholas (right) is located in the town centre and dates back to the 12th century.

WITHERNSEA There are breathtaking views of Withernsea and the surrounding countryside from the town's distinctive lighthouse. This landmark was constructed in the middle of the town because of worries about coastal erosion. Adjoining the lighthouse is Withernsea Lighthouse Museum with a collection which includes Victorian and Edwardian photographs of the area. The Fifties' film star Kay Kendall was born in Withernsea and there is a memorial to her. Her grandfather, Robert Drewery, was the coxswain of the last rowing lifeboat and helped to lay the foundations of the lighthouse.

SPURN POINT Situated on the north bank of the entrance to the river Humber, Spurn Point is a unique place. This three-mile long finger of land snakes out into the Humber estuary and is constantly being reshaped by coastal erosion. Spurn Point is an important location for shipping as it is the home of the Humber lighthouse (below), Humber pilots and the VTS (Vessel Traffic Services). The distinctive black and white lighthouse is no longer in use. Spurn Bird Observatory was opened to visitors in 1946 and provides birdwatchers with the ideal place from which to observe migrating birds.

THE HUMBER BRIDGE This was designed and built to cross the last major estuary without a bridge in Britain. The north tower of this beautiful suspension bridge is sited on the high-water line and the south tower founded in shallow water 1,650ft (500m) from the shore. It is an amazing example of engineering and was developed from a design originally used for the Severn Bridge. The Humber Bridge was built to serve the communities of north Lincolnshire and Humberside. Local businesses and industry in towns such as Immingham and Grimsby have benefited from links to the port of Hull and motorway connections to Manchester, Leeds and Liverpool.

THE DEEP The gleaming glass and aluminium marine life centre called The Deep (right) opened in 2002. Designed by architect Sir Terry Farrell it stands at the confluence of the rivers Hull and Humber and is part of the vision of regeneration for the city of Hull. It was conceived to entertain and educate its visitors about the world's oceans and is a popular visitor attraction and a spectacular landmark.

HULL Although Hull is not mentioned in the Domesday Book people were trading from the point where the river Hull joins the river Humber long before 1066. By the middle ages a port had developed on the west bank of the river and defensive walls were constructed to the west and north. Because of its growing status Edward I granted a charter in 1299 and from then on the town was known as "Kingston on Hull". The Hull marina complex (above), was constructed in 1983 and occupies the site of the former Humber and Railway docks. Located in the heart of the city, today the marina is a haven for sailing craft and yachts of all types and provides over 250 permanent berths. The large black boat on the right is the old Spurn Light Boat. On Princess Dock Street is Hull Trinity House School, which opened in February 1787. It had 36 pupils and the headmaster was the Revd T O Rogers (1787–1789), curate of nearby Sculcoats Church. There was no set curriculum initially but there is no doubt that arithmetic and navigation were among the main subjects. The motto over the door reads *spes super sydera*, which means "hope beyond the stars".

The Vale of York

The rural heart of Yorkshire – a farming region with many fine market towns and the cathedral city York.

This large region of low-lying, undulating countryside stretches from the river Tees in the north to Selby in the south and from the eastern edge of the Yorkshire Dales in the west to the Howardian Hills and the Yorkshire Wolds in the east. It is a rich agricultural area with hay meadows along the river floodplains and large fields elsewhere intensively cultivated for arable crops. There are scattered small woods and larger conifer plantations on sandy soils. The farmhouses and villages are built of a distinctive mottled brick with pantile roofs. The Vale of York is an important transport corridor containing the A1 and A19 trunk roads and the East Coast mainline railway connecting London with Edinburgh. The region includes the busy market towns of Northallerton, Knaresbrough and Thirsk, the elegant spa town of Harrogate and the cathedral cities of York and Ripon.

YORK'S HISTORY Sited at the confluence of the rivers Ouse and Foss, this ancient city has had a turbulent history. Founded by the Romans, it suffered Viking invasion, was ravaged by William the Conqueror and became a major Royalist stronghold during the English Civil War. The city's eventful past is reflected in the many important historic buildings packed within its city walls: attractions such as York Minster (below), the narrow medieval streets around its core which include the famous Shambles, together with the Jorvik Viking Centre and the York Castle Museum have made the city one of the most popular tourist destinations in Britain. York has the longest and best-preserved town walls in Europe and there are 45 towers and four gateways (or "bars") at intervals along its length. A walk along the top of the wall is an ideal way to view the city.

LENDAL BRIDGE This elegant iron bridge (left), with stone towers at either end, was built by Thomas Page in 1863. It is one of nine bridges over the river Ouse in York and links the railway station with York Minster. Before the bridge was built, a ferry ran between the two stone towers, Lendal tower to the east and Barker tower to the west.

YORK MINSTER The largest Gothic cathedral in northern Europe, York Minster is the seat of the archbishop of York, the second highest office in the Church of England. There has been a church here since 627; work on the current Minster began in 1220 and was not completed until 1472. York Minster is famous for the Great East window, completed in 1408, the largest expanse of medieval stained glass in the world. The view above looks up to the ceiling of the Transept Tower.

The city of York was founded by the Romans in AD71. Then known as Eboracum, the city was the capital of Roman Britain. Outside the Minster is a statue of Constantine who was proclaimed Roman Emperor in York in 306.

BOOTHAM BAR The statue of local artist William Etty (right) stands in front of the City Art Gallery looking towards Bootham Bar, the north-western gate of the city, with the grand York Minster in the distance. Large parts of the city wall still exist along with four gatehouses or "bars". In peacetime the bars were designed to restrict traffic and make the work of collecting tolls easier; in times of war, they helped to protect against potential armed invaders. Bootham Bar was partially rebuilt in the 14th and 18th centuries but it still has stonework dating back to the 11th century when it was first erected.

YORK ABBEY The ruins of St Mary's abbey (above and left) lie to the west of York Minster in the Yorkshire Museum gardens. Close to the city centre, this is the ideal spot for visitors and office-workers to relax and enjoy the beautiful gardens. The Benedictine abbey was founded in 1055 and was once the richest Benedictine establishment in the north of England. In 1539, the monastic community was disbanded and the abbey destroyed during the Dissolution. All that remain today are the north and west walls and St Mary's tower in the north-west corner of the abbey. The abbey precinct wall forms part of the town wall of York.

CLIFFORD'S TOWER

This distinctive stone fortification (left) in Tower Street is all that remains of the 13th and 14th century keep of York Castle. In 1190, a mob began to attack the city's Jewish residents and, fearing for their lives, 150 people took refuge in the wooden tower which then occupied this site. After a few days, the militia attempted to break the siege and in the confusion that followed a fire broke out and a local mob invaded the tower. All of the Jews inside the tower were killed by the flames or decided to commit suicide rather than surrender to the mob.

YORK ATTRACTIONS One of York's highlights is the Shambles (far left), a meandering medieval street leading up to the Minster. Today it is filled with souvenir shops; in the Middle Ages it was home to many butchers (the name Shambles comes from the Anglo-Saxon words *shammels* or *fleshshammels* – meaning an open-air slaughterhouse). Most of the buildings along the Shambles are medieval but there are also some outstanding Tudor half-timbered houses. The Shambles is so narrow that some of the upper floors of the houses almost touch. York's historic Guildhall (left) on the banks of the Ouse, behind the Mansion House, dates from the 15th century. One of the city's newest attractions is the observation wheel in the grounds of the National Railway Museum which gives spectacular views over the city.

CASTLE HOWARD One of Britain's finest historic houses, Castle Howard (above) 15 miles north-east of York was built to a design by John Vanbrugh from 1699-1712 and is set amongst magnificent parkland. This opulent residence is, along with Blenheim near Oxford, regarded as a masterpiece of English Baroque architecture. The house took over a century to complete spanning the lifetime of three of the Earls starting with the third Earl of Carlisle who started the project at the beginning of the 18th century. The Earl's choice of Vanbrugh – a dramatist with no previous experience of architecture – surprised many of his contemporaries but the final result can hardly be criticised. Castle Howard gained fame with television audiences when it was used as the setting for *Brideshead Revisited*, the 1981 adaptation of Evelyn Waugh's celebrated novel.

SELBY This attractive market town lies 12 miles south of York along the river Ouse. In the past, Selby was an important shipbuilding centre and harbour thanks to the Selby Canal which linked the town with Leeds. The town is dominated by Selby abbey (above) founded by the Benedictines in 1069, and modelled on Durham cathedral. It is one of the largest parish churches in Britain and is famed for the 14th century Washington window which features the heraldic arms of the ancestors of George Washington, first president of the USA. The design has three red stars above two red bands and is said to be the model for the American flag.

HARROGATE The first mineral spring was discovered at the Tewitt Well in this North Yorkshire town in 1571. By the 18th century, Harrogate had become a fashionable spa to rival Bath and Buxton. The Royal Pump Room (right) has now been converted into a museum telling its story. It is possible to visit the sulphur wells where more than 15,000 people would come for treatments. Next to the museum is Valley Gardens where many of the wells

were found. Today it is one of Harrogate's gorgeous public parks. Originally built in 1806 as Harrogate's first spa building, the Mercer Gallery (top) is now home to the district's superb collection of fine art. The building includes the beautifully restored Promenade Room. Bettys & Taylors opened its first "continental-style tea room" (left) on Parliament Street, overlooking the colourful Montpellier Gardens, in 1919. Since then the company has started another Bettys Tea Room in Harrogate at Harlow Carr and in a number of other Yorkshire towns.

HARLOW CARR The 58 acre garden at Harlow Carr (right) in Crag Lane rivals Wisley in Surrey. It is one of four highly regarded gardens in England run by the Royal Horticultural Society (RHS). Harlow Carr contains an Alpine house and kitchen garden.

KNARESBOROUGH The beautiful town of Knaresborough grew up around the steep sides of the gorge of the river Nidd. This has been a strategic point for centuries and during the Middle Ages Knaresborough was firmly established on the royal circuit. The Norman castle (below) was used as a hideout by the four knights who murdered Thomas à Becket in 1170. It was badly damaged during the Civil War when the Parliamentarians besieged the Royalists here; a Parliamentary decree in 1646 ordered its destruction and many buildings in the town centre are constructed from "castle stone". The castle's remains are open to the public and its grounds are used as a performance space – in particular for events during the Knaresborough Festival every August. The dramatic viaduct across the gorge (right) which everyone associates with the town was completed in 1851.

NEWBY HALL Sir Christopher Wren guided the design of Newby Hall (left), near Ripon, built in 1697. Since 1748 it has been home to the Compton family, whose ancestor William Weddell bought the property and enlarged it during the 1760s. The interior was remodelled by a variety of architects, including Robert Adam, and it is an exceptional example of 18th century interior design. The present grounds were laid out in the 1920s, with herbaceous borders and a dramatic broad grass walk leading down to the river Ure. In 2007 Newby Hall was used for the filming of the television adaptation of Jane Austen's novel *Mansfield Park*. Still privately owned, the house and gardens are open to the public from March to September.

NORTHALLERTON This market town stands in the centre of the Vale of York and has long been an important centre of communications between north and south. Due to its strategic position, Northallerton has often served as a base for armies in times of war. During the Civil War the town was a Royalist stronghold and in 1641 Charles 1 stayed at Porch House (middle right), one of Northallerton's oldest houses built in 1584. Later the town was a resting place for the Duke of Cumberland's troops in their campaign against the Jacobites. Today the town has a thriving market and useful shops – Barker's department store with its distinctive clock over the entrance (top right) has been trading for over 125 years. All Saints church, at the northern end of the High Street, has pews made by the famous workshop of Robert Thompson, the "Mouse Man of Kilburn", and decorated with his distinctive trademark emblem (right). The pretty village of Danby Wiske lies five miles to the north-west. The beautiful parish church (below) stands amidst the fields on the edge of the village and dates from the 12th century.

THIRSK Built around an impressive medieval market square (right) which hosts a twice-weekly open-air market, the lively town of Thirsk lies south of Northallerton overlooking the Hambledon Hills and close to the North York Moors. The church of St Mary is over 500 years old. A plaque (below) marks the birthplace of Thomas Lord who founded Lord's cricket ground; his home now houses Thirsk Museum. Thirsk's most famous recent resident was the author James Herriot (the pen name of James Alfred Wight) who practised as a vet at 23 Kirkgate, now home to the World of James Herriot Museum. Herriot's semi-autobiographical stories – known as the *All Creatures Great and Small* novels – tell of the eventful life of a small-town vet living and working on the edge of the North York Moors.

SUMMER SHOWS Agricultural shows, large and small, have been both great social occasions and the lifeblood of agricultural communities throughout the county for generations. The grandest of these is the Great Yorkshire Show, which is held over three days at the showground on the edge of Harrogate. Equally important are the local shows that are eagerly awaited throughout the year and are organised by show committees in minute detail over many months. The Malton Show (above), for example, has been going strong for more than 120 years. The Aldborough and Boroughbridge Show (below) was first held more than 90 years ago. The Ripley Show, held in the grounds of Ripley Castle, includes falconry displays and racing terriers.

South Yorkshire

A region with a proud history of heavy engineering dominated by the city of Sheffield and the towns of Barnsley, Rotherham and Doncaster.

South Yorkshire ranges from high, bleak moorlands in the west, covered in heather and blanket bog, through the densely populated Coal Measure country containing the city of Sheffield and the towns of Barnsley and Rotherham, to the fertile agricultural country of the Magnesian Limestone belt, and then stretches beyond Doncaster to the east to the Humberhead Levels only a few feet above sea level. It is a many-layered landscape created by the endeavours of people using its resources over many thousands of years to make a living and create farmsteads, villages and urban and industrial settlements, large and small. Yet this densely populated region contains many architectural and landscape gems. These include fine medieval, 18th century and Victorian buildings, public parks and country houses with their surrounding park-lands and gardens. In the west there are large sweeps of open country and tracts of attractive walled, hedged and wooded farmed countryside.

SHEFFIELD The centre of Sheffield is dominated by the Town Hall, built of Derbyshire sandstone, standing at the junction of Surrey Street and Pinstone Street. Designed by EW Mountford, it was described by Sir Nikolaus Pevsner as "a large picturesque pile". It was opened by Queen Victoria in 1897, who was greeted by Sheffield's first lord mayor, the Duke of Norfolk. Two friezes carved in stone adorn the exterior walls; they depict, among other things, grinders, smiths, smelters and miners. The 200ft tower (left) is surmounted by an 8ft high bronze statue of Vulcan, the Roman god of fire and furnaces, with his right foot on an anvil and pincers in his left hand. Inside is a lifesize statue of the Duke of Norfolk and a bust of Queen Victoria. The Peace Gardens (below) in Pinstone Street in front of the Town Hall provide welcome green space in the heart of the city. The latest addition to Sheffield's public green spaces is the Winter Garden, opened in December 2002. It houses 150 species of plants mainly from the northern hemisphere.

HIGH STREET, SHEFFIELD

Leading from the site of the castle and the market area towards the parish church (now the cathedral), High Street (above) has always been an important commercial street since the founding of a town in Norman times. In the right background can be seen Kemsley House, the Sheffield Telegraph building, completed in 1916 and faced with white faience. In the left foreground is the former John Walsh's department store, which was rebuilt after the Second World War to replace the original store opened in 1899 but destroyed in the Blitz in 1940. The Supertram is on its way to the Meadowhall Shopping Centre with 270 stores and parking for 12,000 cars.

THE BOTANICAL GARDENS

The first of Sheffield's public open spaces, the Botanical Gardens (below) opened in 1836. They lie one mile to the west of the city centre. The Botanical Gardens was a forerunner of nearly a dozen public parks that would encircle Sheffield like "pearls on a necklace" and make it into the greenest city in Britain. A competition was held to obtain a design for the gardens, the glass pavilions, entrance and lodges. Robert Marnock won first prize, was appointed curator and laid out the gardens in fashionable "gardenesque" style. Marnock later became curator of the Royal Botanical Gardens in Regent's Park, London. In 1997 the Botanical Gardens received a £5m award from the Heritage Lottery Fund leading to complete restoration of the gardens and pavilions to their former splendour. The garden has a restored bear pit which was home to two live bears until the 1870s.

SHEFFIELD CATHEDRAL The church of St Peter and St Paul (above), Sheffield's medieval parish church, became Sheffield cathedral in 1914. The present church initially dates from the early 15th century, replacing an earlier church probably of early 12th century origin. The crossing tower surmounted by its crocketed spire is an important local landmark. The Shrewsbury Chapel contains the tombs of the 4th Earl of Shrewsbury (died 1538) lying between his two wives and the 6th Earl of Shrewsbury (died 1590) with his feet resting on a Talbot, a hunting dog bearing the family name. In the churchyard is a monument to James Montgomery (1771-1854), newspaper editor and proprietor, anti-slavery campaigner, poet and hymn writer. He wrote more than 350 hymns, the best known being *Angels from the Realms of Glory*.

SHEFFIELD IN THE PEAK Sheffield is enveloped in the west by very extensive tracts of high moorland and upland pastures rising to more than 1,800ft (550m), all within the modern city boundaries and much of it part of the Peak District National Park. Here, Sheffield has its own "lake district" where the valleys are filled by a number of interlinked reservoirs – the Howden, Derwent and Ladybower reservoirs. No moorland can be bleaker or more beautiful, according to the season, than the Bradfield Moors which stretch westwards from Bradfield village beyond Agden Reservoir reaching in their highest parts to more than 1,500ft (457m).

BRADFIELD VILLAGE There are in fact two villages, Low Bradfield and High Bradfield. Dominating High Bradfield is St Nicholas' parish church (above) one of the largest churches in Hallamshire. The churchyard contains some very old gravestones but most interesting is one dating from 1864 when the nearby Dale Dyke Reservoir burst its banks and the rushing torrent of water, pouring down the Loxley valley towards Sheffield, resulted in the death of 240 people. The gravestone in question is that of James Trickett, his wife and three children who all perished in the flood and the last two lines of the dedication reads: "Whate'er the fault this is most true, The Flood is a warning to me and to you." At the entrance to the churchyard is what is reputed to have been a watch-house built as a lookout point to discourage body-snatchers!

BARNSLEY TOWN HALL

Barnsley's Town Hall (right), sited at the junction of Church Street and Shambles Street at the top of Market Hill, was erected when Barnsley was still the coal capital of South Yorkshire and it dominates the townscape today. Constructed in 1932-33, of white limestone blocks, it was designed by the Liverpool architects, Briggs & Thornely. It replaced the dingy old Town Hall in St Mary's Gate. Its imposing frontage, 21 bays long, is surmounted by a conspicuous clock tower. But it may not have ever had a clock tower – this was omitted from the final design on financial grounds and consent by the town council for its construction was only given at the last minute, four months after the foundation stone was laid. The cost of building and furnishing came to £188,000, an enormous figure in the depression days of the 1930s.

WENTWORTH CASTLE

Wentworth Castle is not a castle and not at Wentworth but at Stainborough. The hall consists of a north-west facing wing built by Sir Gervase Cutler between 1670-72 together with a north-east facing wing in the Baroque style which was finished in the 1720s and a Palladian-style front facing south-east elevation built between 1759-64. In 1948 the house, outbuildings and 60 acres of garden were bought by Barnsley Education Committee. In 1949 it opened as a teacher training college and in 1978 became Northern College.
The grounds of the house hold a Grade 1 listing. It featured in the BBC Television's *Restoration* series. Stainborough Castle (left) is a special feature of the gardens – a recently renovated mock medieval castle.

CLIFTON HOUSE MUSEUM

This stately building (right) in Clifton Park dates from the 1780s and was originally the home of Joshua Walker, son of Samuel Walker, one of the founders of Masbrough Iron Foundry. It is believed that the house was designed by John Carr, the York architect. The Council paid £25,000 for Clifton House and 54 acres of surrounding parkland in 1891 "for the use of the townspeople in perpetuity". It became a museum in 1893. The opening of Clifton Park took place on 25 June, 1891 and it was a splendid royal occasion. The official opening was conducted by the Prince and Princess of Wales (later King Edward VII and Queen Alexandra). Also present, as the leading local figure, was the mayor of Rotherham, Alderman Neill, bedecked in his newly acquired cocked hat and mayoral chain of office (made by local jeweller John Mason).

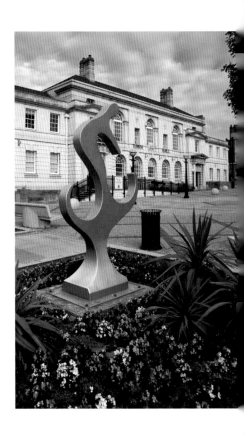

ROTHERHAM Rotherham's origins lie beside an important river crossing, of the river Don, first as a ford and then as a bridge, below its confluence with the river Rother. The bridge chapel (above) is one of only four bridge chapels still surviving in England. Constructed in Rotherham Red sandstone, it was built in the late 15th century and travellers could give thanks for their safe arrival in the town or pray for a safe journey on departure. After the Reformation the chapel was converted into almshouses and then became the town jail and a private residence. By the beginning of the 20th century, to the dismay of many Rotherham citizens, it was used as a tobacconist's shop. The tobacconist was purchased in 1913 and the chapel handed over to the Church Commissioners and re-consecrated by the Bishop of Sheffield in 1924. The old town grew up on the east bank of the river where a low bluff provided a commanding site for All Saints church.

ROCHE ABBEY Situated in the valley of the Maltby Beck nine miles from Doncaster, Roche Abbey was founded in 1147 on a site given by two patrons, Richard de Busli and Richard Fitzurgis. The abbey is on a typical Cistercian site, tucked away in a secluded spot close to a good water supply. Although only an inner gatehouse and the church transepts (right) at the eastern end of the site reach to any height, a complete Cistercian abbey plan can easily be traced in the ruins. In the 1770s Capability Brown was employed by the owner, the Earl of Scarborough, to land-scape the site and he covered up and planted over the ruins of the abbey. The earth and flower beds have now been fully exposed to reveal the full abbey site.

WENTWORTH WOODHOUSE The mansion that can be seen from the park at Wentworth (below) is the East or Palladian front. It was begun by Thomas Watson-Wentworth (later the Marquis of Rockingham) in 1732. It superseded another house facing west built in the florid Baroque style. The Palladian front extends to a length of 606ft (183m), the longest country house front in England. From the village of Wentworth the park is entered beside the Octagon Lodge, one of five surviving lodges. Some visitors entering the park for the first time from this direction are so impressed by the stable block with its clock tower that they think that it is the mansion itself! The 100-strong herd of deer can often be glimpsed grazing among the trees that are scattered throughout the park.

CONISBROUGH CASTLE This magnificent stone castle (above) stands aloft on a tiny "island" of Magnesian Limestone, controlling an important crossing point on the river Don. Dominating all is the stone keep, a massive cylindrical tower, nearly 99ft (30m) high with walls 15ft (4.6m) thick. Attached to the basic cylinder shape are six splayed buttresses which rise to become turrets. By Elizabethan times the castle was in disrepair and was never garrisoned during the Civil War of the 1640s. This saved it from destruction. Now the floors of the keep have been reinstated and the conical roof is once more in place.

BRODSWORTH HALL South Yorkshire has a rich heritage of country houses, parks and gardens. Brodsworth Hall (right), five miles north-west of Doncaster, is a fine Italianate-style country house, of Magnesian Limestone, built and furnished between 1861-63 for Charles Sabine Augustus Thellusson. The house and grounds remained in family ownership until 1990 when they were acquired by English Heritage. After a five-year programme of restoration and conservation they were opened to the public in 1995. The house was designed by Chevalier Casentini. As far as is known Casentini never came to South Yorkshire and his designs were executed by a little-known architect called Philip Wilkinson.

CUSWORTH HALL AND PARK

William Wrightson (1676-1760) was the owner responsible for the building of Cusworth Hall (left and right). The Rotherham mason-architect, George Platt, began to supervise the building of the new hall and on his death in 1742, his son, John, took over. Later extensions were designed by James Paine, the Palladian-style architect. William Wrightson's son-in-law, John Battie-Wrightson, commissioned Richard Woods, the landscape gardener, to improve the 100 acres of grounds surrounding the new hall between 1750-53. Features of the landscaped park dating from this period include three lakes, a bridge, a grotto-like boathouse and a cascade. The park and the house now belong to Doncaster Metropolitan Borough Council, the house having become a museum in 1967. The house and park underwent restoration between 2004-07.

TICKHILL This historic town is perhaps the most pleasant small town in South Yorkshire. Its centre has the air of an ancient market town unaffected by industrialisation. This atmosphere is enhanced by the fact that the town centre has two rookeries and the churchyard is carpeted with celandines in early spring. Yet Tickhill did not grow naturally from an ancient village into a market town – it was an artificial foundation, a planned medieval town established by its Norman lord to serve his estate and his main residence, Tickhill castle. The name Tickhill is derived from the name "Tica's hill", a natural hill that formed the bottom part of the motte on which the Norman castle was built. Tickhill is now dominated by St Mary's parish church (left), one of the outstanding Perpendicular churches in South Yorkshire. It is built of Magnesian Limestone and both inside and outside can only be described as stately. It contains magnificent stone tombs, stone coffins, iron-bound wooden chests and medieval stained glass. Two other unusual buildings are the market or butter cross and St Leonard's Hospital, a timber-framed building dating from 1478. The hospital was founded as a leper hospital in 1225 and its original site was probably in the marshes to the east of the town.

First published in 2010 by Myriad Books Limited
35 Bishopsthorpe Road
London SE26 4PA

Photographs and text © 2010 John Potter and Melvyn Jones

ISBN 1 84746 350 9
EAN 978 1 84746 350 0

Designed by Jerry Goldie Graphic Design

Printed in China